WTC Volunteers America United

By

Ricardo Felix Espinoza

ISBN: 1-4033-5007-8 (e-book)
ISBN: 1-4033-5008-6 (Paperback)

This book is printed on acid free paper.

Partial proceeds of book sales will go to several charities including Riley Children's Hospital, Children's last wish fund, International Association of Firefighters, NY Fraternal Order of Police, Task Force One Firefighters for equip., Indpls, Antique Fire Truck Vehicles, and a student scholarship fund for Holy Rosary school in my mother's name.

1stBooks - rev. 03/10/03

ACKNOWLEGEMENTS

I would like to thank my sisters Connie Hamm, and Sylvia Clark for their expert advise on computers when I was and still am in the learning phase of using a computer.

I appreciated the time they took to trouble shoot the problems I ran into.

I would also like to thank from the bottom of my heart, Fellow patriots Tim, Joey, and Jeremy Derloshon for their expert printing work at HOBBY COPY of Indianapolis.

I would also like to thank fellow volunteer Philip Devan for donating some of his pictures to this project.

Also thanks to Capt. James Twiss for sending me the list of names of his 22 man and woman EMS, Law Enforcement, Firefighters, and Search and Rescue Team from the Pine Ridge Reservation that were involved as volunteers in New York during the month of September of 2001.

Also thanks to Creator Syndicate of Los Angeles for allowing me to use artwork by Indianapolis Star and News artist Gary Varvel.

And most of all I would like to thank my most trusted musician friend Brenda Mazerolle who has encouraged me from the beginning and was someone to talk to when depression and the devil was trying to get the best of me, without her trust, confidence, and assurance, this book might have taken longer to produce.

America United

Oh brothers and sisters, Do not cry,
though we fallen into the dust and flames.
We shall rise and triumph and overcome this scar in time.
Not with despair, though these days do warrant.
We will find our lost souls and gain strength in spirit.
Stone by stone through the dust we will dig,
and pray peace for the fallen, They will hear.
Then turn to the soul of this nation most dear.
Justice will be swift for the evil of blame
We will find you, every one of you, to give you the same.
The spirit of America is coming to you
For we fear you not. Never have, never will
and justice will prevail.

This poem is dedicated to America and it's allies
By Ricardo Felix Espinoza [Ricky Lee]
copy right 2002

[SOULS OF SEPTEMBER]

It was Tuesday morning and I'll always remember
The souls that were lost in that month of September
I went to school and took the test
But when I heard the news I had to rest
My body was hurting the Goosebumps were rising
And then I started thinking of all who were dying
I saw the Firemen, Police, and the nation was crying
But we got back on our feet and kept on trying
I wanted to believe that it was all just a lie
But I knew it wasn't because of the smoke in the sky
I knew that we would show evil that good shall overcome
Because of all the new angels that had risen above.

By Matt Barton
Sophomore Student at Center Grove High School Of Indianapolis IN.
This poem is dedicated to those who lost their lives Sept. 11, 2001

One morning as I was waiting with other workers to go to work. We were sitting on the four foot brick wall that sits in front of the Javits Center when a blue police transport bus pulls up in front of us and several Firefighters stepped out and a few walked to my right towards the food tent and a few Firefighters appeared to be painfully walking to my left to sit on the wall next to us. These men had just returned from a work shift at Ground Zero so we told them to sit down and rest and the one that appeared to be the youngest and had a darker complexion said my feet are burning up as he struggled to put one foot in front of the other. I stepped off the wall and walked up to him and I said come on sit down and rest, take it easy, and the firemen said, [I need some water, I got to drink some water first,] and I said [I'll get you some water just sit down and rest,] and the Fireman said [That's all right I can get it] and I said [Look! I came all the way from Indianapolis Indiana to help you firemen so at least let me bring you some water,] The fireman looked at me and I could almost see a tear glisten in his eyes and then he said [Okay] I said [I'll be right back and I ran eighty feet to the tent that stored the donated quart bottles of water on ice.

I returned and gave all three Firefighters a cold bottle of water which they drank with gusto, then one of the volunteers named Chris wanted to take a couple of pictures of me with the Firefighters as they quenched their thirst And I asked them what their names were so I can write to them or send them a post card when I get home.

Billy Eisengrien, George Johnson, and Dan McWilliams they all had a total look of exhaustion and I could tell they did appreciate our help. Well as it turned out, earlier that day these three Firemen had their picture taken by a photographer as they displayed an American flag and that picture became the most famous picture of Firefighters in the world and soon became a US stamp.

INTRODUCTION

My name is Ricardo Felix Espinoza, and several years ago, during a talent show which I was in charge of, at a local night club called THE GROVE, in Beech Grove, Indiana, A group of local musician friends of mine, From the band, [Pure Gold] nicknamed me Ricky Lee, and it stuck.

The guys found it hard to pronounce, or remember my last name every time I was introduced on stage, I didn't mind the nickname, mostly because it was easier for them to pronounce, and easier for everyone to remember. I got so used to the name that I used it as the heading on my business cards of my sign designing business.

Also several years ago the Pure Gold Band, and I called up some of our musician friends in Indianapolis to play for a benefit which I was in charge of organizing for two Firefighters that were killed in a devastating back draft fire, at the Athletics Club on Meridian Street in Indianapolis.

The benefit was held at the original Grove Nite Club on Emerson Ave, In Beech Grove on a Sunday afternoon with a variety of bands playing music such as, Oldies, Country, Rock, Blues, R&B Soul, and our feature guest was a national recording artist, Henry Lee Summer,

The turnout was tremendous, With standing room only, From twelve noon, till midnight, With an all out finale at the end of the evening, and musicians from different bands completely filling the stage, me on the congas, and Henry Lee Summers on drums. The benefit helped raised $ 5,000 for the Firefighters Union.

This book is dedicated to the gallant Firefighters like John J. Lorenzano, and Ellwood M. Gelenius, [Woody] Also Fire Department Chief Peter Ganci, First Deputy Fire Commissioner William [Bill] Feehan, Father Mychal Judge, and the 343 other fire fighters of the FDNY, also the NYPD, PAPD Medical EMS, and civilians that lost their lives at the World Trade Center.

Ellwood M. Gelenius, (Woody)

John Joesph Lorenzano

It's also dedicated to every American, and to my home state of Indiana, and the city of Indianapolis.

I've been fairly successful as a sign painter, and a commercial artist. And in 1966 my father bought me a white pearl drum set, and one week later, I was the drummer for the only Tex - Mex Conjunto Band in Indianapolis, then after serving in the Air Force, I moved to

Corpus Christi Texas, and became a lead singer with a ten piece, Latino orchestra, We were called Chicano Pride band.

And after eight and a half years, I moved back to Indy because my mother was diagnosed with breast cancer and died about one year later.

I never returned to Corpus Christi, Texas, because I wouldn't have been able to visit my mothers grave site when I wanted to.

So I became a singer for a few years in Indianapolis, with a top forty country and southern rock band called [Ricky Lee & The Dusters] I also sing soft, and classic rock, and oldies, and being raised during the 60's Motown era, I've developed a touch of Latin soul in my singing, and in my song writing. [Well, At least I think so.]

I was born in Indianapolis Indiana, and I am proud to say, I am a proud Hispanic Mexican American Hoosier, with six sisters and one brother, We were basically raised on the east side of the center of Indianapolis, where I attended school #74, during preschool at the age of five, and school # 9 through the eighth grade, and through most of those years, My father owned and managed his own Mexican food market, which was the first and only Mexican food store in Indianapolis, The store was called, [El Nopal Food Market] Which means [The Cactus Food Market] I also learned to fine tune my social skills as a salesman in that store, At the age of twelve, I was Shinning shoes for customers, and drawing pencil portraits for two dollars per person. And even though my father, and my mother, owned and run the store, My dad Feliciano Espinoza also worked long hard hours as a Track man, and Railroad supervisor for Conrail Railroad, which was originally I.U. Railroad, And how my dad found the time to organize and become the founder of the first job training and education center for the Hispanic community of Indianapolis is beyond me.

My father has even kept in touch with former mayor of Indianapolis, Senator Richard Lugar, whom my father supported during Lugars run for Mayor of Indianapolis, which he won I believe with the help of the Hispanic community vote.

My Father and Mother taught us all to be proud of our heritage, and respect people and their religion. And they were also very generous in helping the poor families, and it didn't matter what their race or color was.

My parents would help anyone who needed help, even allowing credit at the store for the families that we had come to know, And in those days, Hispanic families went through some difficult times, But that was just part of adjusting to a new life in a new town, and for some people, It was adjusting to a new country.

We've even experienced some of the harsh racial realities of the time, in the 60's, And at that young age, I didn't know or realize that the African American population was fighting for not only human rights, But also their right to vote, and they eventually got that right,

A lot of things were beginning to change back in the 60's, socially and politically.

From the music of the time, to the way people dressed and even the hair styles, And, Man,! Have they changed, Who would have thought that walking down the street with your pants hanging half way off your rear end would be in style for some kids.

Or bright green, yellow, purple, and blue hair would be the new style of the 21st century for some kids.

Back in the early sixties you would have been run out of town or expelled from school for any one of these changes of style.

But the Hispanic community basically got along with all races in our society, and I've always been proud of my family, and all the things each one of them has accomplished in their lives. With three sisters in the Air Force, U.S. Navy, and Marines, Paula, Air Force retired, Isabel, [Cha-Cha] U.S Navy, was part of general Shwartskof's staff during the Desert Storm days, and Connie a U.S Marine and computer specialist, Consuelo, with her own beauty salon, and the twins Sylvia, a program support assistant at the Richard L. Roudebush, Medical Center, and Olivia, a cake designer, which as an artist, I found very interesting, And then there was my brother Graciano, [Hector,] or [Chano], who found his spot as a foreman with a local construction company.

I started my freshman year in 1968 at Arsenal Tech High School and towards the end of my senior year, I enlisted into the Air Force and served my country as a heavy equipment operator.

I would have preferred military police as a career, But that school was already filled, And there was a need of construction equipment operators that were running snow removal equipment at Pease, Air Force base in Portsmouth New Hampshire, So guess where I ended up,

And even though I was not really happy with the career field I was placed into, I tried to adapt to this way of life for four years. My sister Paula, was the one who, while on a tour of duty in Hawaii, talked me into enlisting into the Air Force, [Come on Rick join the Air Force, Look at me, tropical Islands, the beeches, the hot summer climate,] Yeah I remember that sales pitch every time I stepped in front of the snow plow I was driving and I had to change the shear pins on the plow blade in the winter of 71, 72, 73, and 74. Plowing snow to the side of the runway left walls of snow 13ft high.

Yeah I remember them blizzards well.

But I was proud to serve my country, and it was a good thing I enlisted into the R.O.T.C program. at Arsenal Tech high school, It not only prepared me for the rigors of military life, but it also taught me discipline, and why we should respect the military uniform, and what it represents, Honor, Respect, Dignity.

When I attended the military ball at Arsenal Tech, with my date Alisha Fonseca I thought that was the proudest moment of my life.

Then years later nothing could compare to how proud I felt when my first son was born and he got the same nickname I had when I was in school, [Rico]

But when I became a member of the volunteer team that converged in New York City's Manhattan Island, to assist the city, and my country, in anyway I possibly could in the search and rescue operation effort, That, was a feeling of pride of a different kind, unmatched, that was felt by every other volunteer that had arrived from every part of the country.

We were not Fireman, EMS, or Policeman, And I wasn't working with the city in any official capacity, I was from the civilian sector, of this country, and in my heart, Just being there, was something, as an American, I just had to do.

Rick Espinoza

CHAPTER ONE

DISASTER

The devastation in New York City was incredible and beyond comprehension, There were thousands of people buried in the rubble, and many were running out of time and air to breath and survive. Time was very crucial to the people buried, and to the people that were digging them out, Every second, minute, day, and week, was a matter of life and death for each of the victims, Thousands of Americans were trapped or stuck in thousands of different situations with the extreme heat and smoke from the fire slowly suffocating them.

The disaster in New York city, left it's leaders with a mission of tremendous proportion, Not only for mayor Rudolph Giuliani, and Governor George Pataki.

But for almost every public service employee within the area of destruction. They were going to have to work as if in a war zone, By removing and clearing the debris, Searching for any possible survivors, Identifying the dead, which in many cases was almost impossible, due to the conditions of many of the bodies, Comparing identification descriptions from relatives, with the bodies or parts that were found, And then organizing search crews, controlling crowds, and traffic, and securing a safe perimeter several blocks away from the disaster area. Hundreds of people were incinerated to ashes from the tremendous heat and would never be found.

Then locating an area to haul all the steel and debris, Organizing a temporary morgue, and a forensics area to identify and confirm the dead, Securing the city, and nations airports subways, and government facilities And lets not forget the food to feed the rescue crews, and the hundreds of semi-trailers with donations from all over the country with thousands of tons of food, drinking water, and supplies that were desperately needed for the firemen and rescue teems, Keep in mind that everything that was shipped in, had to be unloaded and separated, and many times, Had to be reloaded and unloaded at still another location,

Then to top it off, there were rumors that any one of the trucks we were unloading could be booby-trapped with a bomb that could blast a hole, the size of a large swimming pool, P.S. That in itself had us all on edge every time we opened the rear doors of the trailers when we did start to work.

And at times it was kind of funny when as I held my breath and unlocked the rear doors I would look back and see a couple of guys plugging their ears with their fingers and closing their eyes as they stood only four feet away.

I would giggle to myself as I realized that if the rumors were true, the sight of them, might be the last thing I may see in this lifetime.

New York University's downtown medical center which was the closest to the disaster area became swamped with dead and injured, And amputation decisions had to be made carefully and quickly, Also several emergency triage tents for injured rescue workers had to be set up.

Many of the rescue workers were injured as they slipped in the mud or off the wet steel beams.

Many were treated for heat exhaustion, and dust in their eyes which was very dangerous since much of the dust was mixed with asbestos, cement, fiberglass, and glass powder.

Much of the Trade Center Towers glass disintegrated into powder when the towers came down,

Dozens of firefighters were treated and pulled out of ground zero due to eye injury, Then there were the fires, coming from underground called Hot Spots which were generating heat all along the steel beams, that were on top of the rubble, Some steel beams were so hot, that it melted the soles of the boots if you stood in one place, a minute to long. Also there were sections where any place a worker stepped on could cave in, which is what eventually happened to several firefighters that were promptly dug out and lifted to safety.

From the time I turned on the television set on the morning of September 11, 2001, and witnessed the second plane hit the south tower on live television, to the time I boarded the Grey Hound bus to New York City, I kept track of everything that happened in my notebook journal.

I was on my way to the most incredible experience of my life but, I wasn't going alone,

I was going to New York city with the spirit of all the people of Indianapolis and America that wanted to be there to help but due to family and job obligations, couldn't go,

I was going to be their eyes and ears, and I was also going to witness first hand, the Solidarity, Unity, and True Power of the American Spirit.

This is my story…

During her campaign while running for Congress, I had the honor of interviewing Julia Carson, and with the extra votes from the Hispanic community she won the election campaign.

As the bus neared the Lincoln Tunnel someone said there's Ground Zero! and you could see the white trail of smoke drifting from the disaster area.

Shortly after arriving into New York City I had my first glimpse of the disaster area which was four blocks away from the security blockade barrier.

After meeting other volunteers I was invited to camp out with them.

CHAPTER TWO

ON A MISSION

September 11,2001 which was a Tuesday, will live in my mind for the rest of my life, It is the day I woke up and turned on the television to check on the weather, It was a routine I've done for several years, to make sure I would be able to deliver or pick up a plastic advertising sign, I was also working part-time with my landlord Don, and his gutter business.

But As the TV came on, I noticed what appeared to be a building burning, and at first, I thought the fire was in the city county building in downtown Indianapolis, and as the camera in the helicopter zoomed away from the building, I realized that the fire was in New York city,

The Today show with Matt Laur, and Katie Couric was on, and it was mentioned that a plane had just crashed into one of the towers of the World Trade Center, and there was some question, and some doubt that this was an accident.

People were running for their lives down below as giant sections of glass and debris fell and crashed onto the pavement.

The first thing I noticed was that the sky was perfectly clear, So I wondered why the pilot didn't see the towers, That was the first thing that went through my mind, and I thought this couldn't have been an accident.

It wasn't like July 28,1945, when a B-25 Bomber accidentally got lost in the fog and crashed into the 79th floor of the Empire State Building, and fourteen people lost their lives, And still, that building held, They say, They just don't build them like they used to, when they talk about cars, And maybe the same applies to the construction of sky scrapers.

The Empire State Building, In its design, and construction was solid, especially on the outside of the building.

Had the Empire State Building been built like the Trade Center towers, There would have been a lot more lives lost, And the plane could have possibly passed through the building or ended up imbedded in the center.

But instead, The B 25 was left protruding, with it's tail section hanging outside of the building.

The World Trade Center Towers were designed and constructed with 43.000 windows covering the outside of the structures. Which created a fragile outer shell covering the building., and as attractive, and impressive as it may have been, maybe the safety of it's occupants was not considered when it was designed,

But then again, No one could have ever dreamed that even a terrorist would have done what happened on Sept, 11, 2001

On September 11, 2001 There were actually four passenger jets that lifted off and headed for their destinations, and all within 43 minutes of each other.

The Boeing 767, Flight 11 with 81 passengers, and 11 crew members had left the Boston airport at 8;00 am, heading for Los Angeles, California, Then at 8;14 am, United Airlines Flight 175, A Boeing 767 departs Boston's Logan Airport, Also heading for Los Angeles, with 56 passengers and 9 crew members.

At 8;21 American Airlines Flight 77 a Boeing 757 took off from Washington DC at Dulles Airport with 58 passengers aboard and 6 crew members, And the fourth hijacked plane, United Airlines flight 93 a Boeing 757, left Newark, New Jersey, at 8;42 am heading for San Francisco, with 38 passengers and 7 crew members aboard,

United Airlines flight 11, crashed into the north tower first, without warning the jet loaded with 20.000 gallons of jet fuel, exploded on impact, You can only imagine what the people within the building saw those last few seconds, as the plane headed straight for them, or what was going on in the plane before impact, Were the passengers in the process of fighting back for control?

The flames incinerated every floor from 90 to 100, No one realized at the time, That this was just the beginning of the most incredible act of terrorism ever inflicted on the United States.

Then eighteen minutes later, I noticed to the right of the screen what appeared to be a plane passing the area, and before I could say another word, the plane plowed into the south tower.

Now, Everyone's eyes and cameras were already focussed on the towers, and viewers across the country and around the world, witnessed the second plane as it plowed into the South tower.

The explosion of jet fuel blasting into a giant intense fireball inside, and outside of the building, with the flames covering twenty floors and completely destroying levels 78 through 87, on impact. And everyone within that location died instantly, If they hadn't gotten out or evacuated the area.

The third hijacked plane, American Airlines flight 77 with 64 passengers, crashed into the west wall, of the E-Ring section of the Pentagon, in Washington DC.

Then at 10;10 am The passengers of United Airlines Flight 93 realized what is going on and decide to go for broke, and charged the hijackers in an attempt to keep them from reaching their target,

The passengers had received word through cell phones about what was going on in New York and in Washington DC, and they suddenly realized what the hijackers objective was,[Suicide].

Even though they didn't know what the target was, They knew, That they had to stop the hijackers at all cost, The struggle had to have been fierce, with the passengers all knowing why they all had to make their move, With deadly force. the American defending passengers were probably just reaching the hijacking pilot in the cockpit, when the hijacker suddenly realized they were not going to reach their target,

They quickly aimed the plane towards the ground, and pushed the throttle at full speed. Witnesses say that the plane picked up speed just before impact on an open field in Shanksville, Pa, Which was about 80 miles from Pittsburgh.

There were 45 people aboard that plane that disintegrated on impact. And the thought on every American at that moment was [Why?].

There are times when I wish I could have been there, just to get my hands on the throat of one of the hijackers, His last word probably would have been, ugagaAla, And mine would have been, J E S U S C H R I S T.

I believe that the terrorist made one BIG mistake when they decided to attack this country.

Maybe its because they were extremely ignorant, or riding them camels in the hot sun to long, But they underestimated the bravery, gallantry, and the determination of the American Spirit.

Because it can't be beat, not in the past, not now, and not in the future, or EVER.

I believe they have been trained to believe that America would always turn the other cheek every time we were slapped in the face with the indignity of terrorist threat or death,

But America is not only strong, America, and it's people are a powerful force when united, And that has always been proven, throughout the history of this country.

On December 7, 1941 when the misled Japanese attacked Pearl Harbor, They awoke the sleeping giant, and paid the price of defeat, with humiliation, which in those days, was worse than death.

Well, this time it wasn't just one giant that awoke, The terrorist awoke the giant in every single American, in the United States and it's allies. The attack brought a whole new meaning to the word

13

Awareness. Many of the people that died during the attacks on September 11, didn't even know why,

Meanwhile in New York, As the second plane ripped through to the other side of the south tower, people and debris were blasted out of the building as the tip of the plane tore through every wall and office space,

The plane then crashed straight through to the other side of the structure, All in less than two seconds.

Also within seconds after the impact many people had to make their last decision in life, either jump out of the broken window, or burn alive, And the heat was so intense that they jumped without any regard to the height or level they were at.

Some had made their decision to jump as they were already on fire, and others made the gallant decision to go together, as they locked arms and jumped. There were bodies of jumpers that leaped from as high as the 60th floor, and their decision to jump, had to be made, within seconds after the planes impact, They just absolutely had no other choice, Either jump or burn.

Some New York firefighters even say that the bodies of the jumpers seemed to explode on impact against the concrete. At least one Firefighter was reported to have been killed by a jumper.

Father Mychal Judge, a chaplain for the New York Fire Department was kneeling by a Firefighter he was giving last rites to, when he was struck in the head and killed by falling debris, The chaplain had made the mistake of taking his helmet off during the prayer, He died instantly.

And as I watched this cowardly attack on our country, I thought of all the people that were still trying to escape through every possible way that was available above the impact area.

Surely the elevators were out of commission, There were 194 passenger elevators that were knocked out instantly, and many people must have died, as they were riding the elevators, heading to or out of the buildings when it was hit.

People above the impact area were trapped by the extreme heat and flames, I actually saw people jumping out from as high as what appeared to be the 80th floor,

I also realized that this day was a mirror image of the day America was caught by surprise at Pearl Harbor.

Like December 7,1941 and 2,403 people were killed. It was also a beautiful day then, The sun was shinning, with a partly cloudy sky, And you could feel the breeze from the bay, But back then, part of the blame was due to [1]The lack of technology of the time, [2]The inexperienced people that were responsible for the information that was relayed to their superiors, And [3] The superiors that didn't take the information serious, when they received it. This was why Pearl Harbor was caught off guard, The signs were there, and the warnings were there, But no one took it seriously, Some one forgot to educate someone, the fact that these enemies were not your everyday soldiers.

The Taliban guerilla fighters were suicide fanatical enemies of their own people, and life itself.

Once again, innocent people have died in America, and their only crime was,

They were Americans.

They were people that died, while working and supporting their families, and making an honest living.

They had no animosity towards any religion, and were caught unaware by cowards that respect no religion, and no ones life, not even their own. They are the lowest life form scum of the earth that have no place in any society on this planet, and should be terminated from this lifetime now and forever.

This was not just an attack on New York city, But on the United States of America,

My Country, And as for me, There was nothing I could do for Pearl Harbor, which happened long before my time, But New York was only hours away by bus,

And as I watched the glass and debris fall down below, I prayed to god that the people that were getting out of the tower, were running as far away from the area as possible.

Then I noticed just briefly through the helicopter camera, that was scanning the area below the towers, That dozens of people were still standing near the building, and looking up at the fire above, which everyone thought was contained.

No one expected, imagined, or realized that they were still in imminent danger.

There were still people standing a half block away and some just outside of the building, And there were people still watching from what they thought was a safe area inside their office building across the street, or from the Burger King nearby,

But when the planes crashed into the towers, the extreme heat from the flames had melted the support beams that held the structure together within the middle of each building, and this caused the towers to crumble and crash towards the ground,

It was the south tower that gave way first, at 9; 50 am The structure seemed to just crumble straight down, and the crowds below had only seconds to run for cover as millions of tons of steel, concrete, and building debris fell to the pavement below.

There were already dead and injured people all around the buildings, and no one could get to the injured, because of the falling debris.

That is no one except the EMS personnel, that not only risked their lives, But died trying to save many of the victims that were injured or unconscious.

Then at 10;28 exactly thirty-eight minutes after the south tower went down, The north tower collapses, with the top section of the tower falling at an angle, and crashing through the weakened floors below,

And as the weight of the building tore through the floors, it caused a banana peel effect, as the walls of the towers broke off with sections of the building one hundred yards in length, Breaking away and falling to the streets, and smashing civilian and emergency vehicles, flag poles, street lights, and parking meters.

Other sections of steel beams fell and impaled themselves like massive arrows of steel into buildings nearby across the street like the bank building that was ripped open right down the middle as the north tower crashed to the ground.

The dust and smoke seemed to travel endlessly., Rescue vehicles and fire trucks were flattened, or destroyed. It was unknown if there were victims inside of several vehicles, due to the fact, that you couldn't even look inside the flattened vehicles, some people had jumped into their vehicles either to escape the falling debris or to back up the vehicle away from danger and were killed from the mega tons of falling concrete, glass, and steel,.

When the smoke and dust began to clear a large portion of the Port Authority Police, Firefighters, NYPD and E.M.S. personnel and civilians were buried in the rubble. The area of destruction was tremendous and covered approximately 14 to16 acres and even further if you count the mess the dust left behind.

The area of the World Trade Center covered about four large city blocks with two towers 110 stories high also a 54 and a 47 story building that all crashed and destroyed the buildings across the street all around the area.

The 47 story building #7 of the trade center collapsed and there were still other nearby buildings that were now burning.

Also the 54 story building at One Liberty Plaza had partially collapsed, This was the NASDAQ, Stock Market's new location and the center of New York and world wide trading,

Firefighters had entered nearby buildings across the street from the towers to evacuate people, before the towers came down and were caught off guard when gigantic sections of the towers crashed against the side of these buildings.

The firemen inside the buildings were knocked from side to side as those buildings began to sway left and right and even knocking firemen down the stairwell as they bounced against the walls.

The dust from the disaster area seemed to travel for miles and the destruction it caused also caught everyone off guard.

The dust flowed through the streets like a giant smoky wave, with extreme heat, like hot volcanic ash, So hot, that it burned hundreds of vehicles it came into contact with, and in some places the extreme heat from the dust not only burned the paint off the cars, but completely gutted every vehicle inside and out, Including taxi, and city buses, and if the dust caught up with a person in that area, it would have burned, the hair off their head, and the cloths and skin off their bodies as they were buried with the hot suffocating concrete dust powder.

When the dust began to settle, the remaining shell shocked FDNY, NYPD, PAPD [Port Authority Police Department] Medical, and civilian personnel, converged on the rubble in a frenzy, trying to find their comrades, brothers, sisters, family members, and friends. The dust was so thick across the ruins, that all you could verily see were ghostly shadows of the other people climbing, searching, screaming and calling out for their people.

The dust [still hot] burned your eyes and it was hard to breath and the heat was still tremendous, and for a few hours it was complete chaos, There were not enough police to guard and protect the property from vandals, crooks, looters, and just plain thieves, and souvenir seekers.

Later it would be discovered that at least 343 Firefighters were buried in the rubble, including a number of NYPD officers, 36 Port Authority Police officers, several medical personnel, volunteer Firemen, and over three thousand innocent civilians.

As the dust began to clear the majority of the civilians that climbed the rubble in search for survivors were gallant and their presence there was honorable.

But there were people, that in the middle of the worst disaster in U.S history, were more concerned about taking souvenirs, or personal property that didn't belong to them, and for a while there weren't enough security or law enforcement officers to stop everyone, It was absolute chaos,

Several people were arrested for looting, and it was reported that even a Port Authority Police officer was arrested for steeling a collection of Rolex watches and jewelry from the rubble and if true, He is the worst disgrace in history to ever wear the PAPD uniform, There were about 36 Port Authority Police officers that died when the towers came down, And how can a man or woman face their friends, and family, after the disgrace of being caught red handed, A law enforcement officer stealing? I just hope when he was locked up they threw away the key.

The National Guard was called in to control the crowd and new steps and restrictions were enforced to protect the property.

Barriers were set in a circular perimeter around the disaster area reaching several blocks away and every place of business, and residence within that area was evacuated. Federal officers were about to take over the entire city to organize security coming in and out of the Manhattan Island area.

And to organize the search and rescue operation, hundreds of details will soon converge on the FEMA officials that will be responsible for the complete emergency plans.

WTC- FACTS

It took two hundred thousand tons of steel to build the World Trade Center, which began it's construction in 1966,

In 1974 French aerialist Philippe Petit had a tightrope stretched between both towers, then at 1,300 feet, actually walked, from one tower to the other, Where he then turned around and walked back to the building he started at which was an incredible act in itself.

Only one man has climbed the side of one of the towers, and one man has jumped from the top of the towers in a parachute.

The buildings also had two observation decks, one on the 107th floor which was inside, and one on the 110th floor which was on the outside, on the very top of the roof, where on a clear day, you can see as far as 55 miles away.

The designer of the World Trade Center Towers, was a Japanese American named Minoru Yamasaki, Born in Seattle in 1912, The buildings weight was over 1.5 million tons, with ten million square feet of space, 198 miles of heating ducts, 23000 white fluorescent light fixtures Also the express elevators traveled 27 feet per second, and could reach the 110th floor in four minutes, ten seconds. There were also 194 passenger elevators in the towers,

The world trade towers had each stood one hundred and ten floors in height, with several floor levels underground.

Also as many as 50,000 employees worked at the World Trade Center.

150,000 people would visit daily as they walked through the Austin J. Tobin Plaza. Levels one, two, and three were -almost all parking garage areas, with a few security offices that had existed until February 26th 1993, when a car bomb blew out a section of the basement in the north tower.

Government and secret service personnel maintained vehicles in the underground lots, and since the 1993 car bombing, The car lot has been closed to all visitors.

There was also a stockpile of freon stored for the air conditioning system and there were several thousand gallons of diesel fuel also in storage.

There was also an underground armory with a bank vault housing 12 tons of gold, and 1000 tons of silver.

The PATH subway trains were 80 feet down in the lowest level and the complete subway area will have to be rebuilt, and perhaps moved to another location of the city.

The office's of Cantor Fitzgerald lost more lives than any other company with about 600 people still missing and presumed dead,

Marsh and McClennon Co, lost 400 employees, And AON Co, reported 200 still missing,

The devastation was horrific and beyond description, And it was going to take men and women working together as a team to sift through every concrete stone bit by bit, piece by piece, And they were all going to work together, through-out the city as one team. When I first saw the towers come crashing down on television I could only imagine the chaos, death and destruction down below where the fire trucks, firemen, police, and all the other medical personnel and civilians were being buried alive by the megatons of steel, concrete glass, and office debris.

My heart was filled with anger, and rage at what was going on, because I couldn't do anything about it.

Granted, I didn't know anyone in New York, But I felt like my own family and friends were being murdered before my eyes.

I listened to the news reports of how the Scumbag Taliban terrorist had planed the deadly assassination of New York city and the American people.

And after listening to reports of volunteers signing up to assist in the rescue operation to find survivors, something touched my heart unlike anything ever in my life.

And on the 5th day after the towers came down, On the 16th of September, 2001, On a Saturday, which was also the day my Aztec Indian artwork was to be on exhibit,

I boarded the Greyhound bus at 6;30 in the morning, destination, GROUND ZERO.

I was verily surviving and trying to make ends meet financially, and I could have used the money I would have made selling my art work, But it seemed like nothing else mattered anymore, not even one of the biggest sign projects I've ever had offered to me to work on.

The money just wasn't important anymore, Even playing music and singing wasn't important any more and music and art was my heart and soul, But then again so was being an American.

The only thing that did matter was that fellow Americans were buried alive and even the Firefighters and official rescue personnel were going to need a helping hand., I was on my way, and nothing was going to stop me in helping in any way I could.

Throughout my trip, towards New York City, I would look out across the country side and I would say to myself [Their not going to get away with this] I also wondered what I would see, when I got there and what the spirit of the people would be like, and what their attitude would be towards strangers.

After all, I wasn't blond with blue eyes, And I also wondered where was I going to sleep, Sure, I had money to hold out for a while, and I had a sleeping bag to sleep in if I couldn't find a room to rent but I had almost forgotten that I was going to be in New York city, where the cost of living is twice as high as Indiana and where movies depict armed robbery so common it seemed like a sport, and I wondered, Was I really going to encounter Lions, Tigers, and Bears?

And were there really pan handlers on every corner?

I soon found out that New York City was nothing Like the movies, at least not as terrible as it was made out to be.

New York City is incredibly beautiful, and breath taking and the people were warm and receptive towards me.

CHAPTER THREE

NEW YORK, NEW YORK

As the bus began to arrive along the bay across from Manhattan Island You could see the skyline of the city with all the buildings standing together majestically, But most of all, You could see the empty space where the towers used to be, and the steady stream of white smoke that marked the location of where the towers used to be, And I thought to myself, That's my destination,

My heart began to pound at the very sight of the actual devastation even at this distance The smoke from the disaster area seemed to travel across the sky for miles towards the south.

Even at this distance across the bay, The thought of knowing that the place I was looking at across the bay, still had thousands of people buried alive, my heart was filled with helpless agony, as I closed my eyes and prayed for the victims and their families.

I had a surge of vengeance flowing through my veins against the scum of the earth that were responsible for this atrocity.

But hopefully there were survivors, This I prayed for, and I mentally called out to the disaster victims, [Hold on, I'm on my way, PLEASE, hold on, PLEASE.]

I know that no matter where each victim was within the rubble, each one of them knew that rescue personnel were on their way, and that they were all digging as fast as they could if they survived long enough, They knew we were coming.

Then as the bus arrived at the station, I quickly gathered my blue duffel bag with cloths, and my sleeping bag which belonged to one of my best friends, Harry Eugene Welch Jr., who loaned it to me.

Now if he had only told me that the zipper was broken, But I took it, cause I had a feeling I was going to need and use it.

I was directed to the subway station, which would of eventually taken me closer to the ground zero area, But due to security precautions at the time, that section of the subway was closed.

The taxi driver stated that there were probably rescue teams searching the subway trains path to see if they could find survivors or get to them. There was a subway train that had entered under the ground zero location, Possibly more than one. I had to take a taxi, and a very polite and kind Muslim gentleman, drove me to as close as he could to the ground zero area.

I arrived near the perimeter blockade about three blocks away since it was so crowed with curious people walking along the streets and I wondered what were they all trying to see? And I soon found out that they were watching the tow trucks pulling out the vehicles and the busses going to and from the disaster site carrying the workers from the disaster area.

Then I noticed that every hotel, store, shop, and restaurant within the four block area had been shut down and evacuated since the attack.,

Crowds had gathered at all the blocked barriers, just to see what they were able to see and take pictures of.

But unless you had a super zoom lens, All you were going to see was people everywhere, there were people from almost every part of the world.

New York in itself is an extremely diverse community, and with reporters from all over the world, roaming throughout the area, It became a spectacle to behold.

Upon arriving in New York I realized that there were not as many people on the streets as I thought there would be.

Then I began to notice the family members or friends of the victims of the World Trade Center, It was a sad sight, and my heart went out to them as they carried flyers with pictures and information about the victims they were looking for.

It was a hopeless situation, and the odds of finding them alive had all but diminished by now and I have a feeling they knew it, but they were in hopeless denial.

One group walked up to me and asked me if I had seen this person and I would look at the picture and say no I haven't not yet, But I am here to work as a volunteer in the search and rescue effort and if I see this person I will call this number and let you know. They would shake my hand and thank me and there eyes seemed to glow with a spark of hopeful excitement just from knowing that I was a volunteer.

But what else could I have said to ease their pain and sadness.

There were other people that openly wept when they would see the families searching for their loved ones, It made you wish you could do or say something, But what could you really say?

The victims friends and families placed the flyers with pictures and information throughout the city on almost every corner within a two mile radius, on cars, trucks, iron light post, windows and walls, and some businesses even allowed them to post pictures on the outside wall of their business.

It seemed everyone was trying to do their part in one way or another and it was greatly appreciated by everyone concerned.

There was a sense of sorrow and sadness in the air, and speaking of air, I also noticed that the air around the area of the blockade which was four blocks from Ground Zero had a strange smell, like lead or something I just couldn't place my finger on it, So I tried an old trick that works every time.

I stuck out my tongue which can taste and sense the flavor or aroma with the thousands of taste buds and suddenly I tasted the foul, lead taste in the air, and it was so bad that it made me yuck with a facial expression to match.

The sky at the time was bright, clear, sunny and warm, and it seemed like a picture perfect day,

Was I the only one that was noticing the air just wasn't right.? Everyone was so busy walking around trying to see what they could see that they didn't seem to notice.

Some couples were carrying their babies in their arms and strollers only four blocks from the disaster site.

Could it be that there was still fallout of asbestos, and lead in the air?, and who knows what else.?

No one realized at the time, that the air could possibly still be contaminated.

Did anyone know? And should the public have been warned if it was true? Was it true? Was there still serious, possible, air contamination that still existed? Maybe we'll never know.

There were rumors That the city was denying a 4.5 measure of asbestos or lead in the air which was considered unacceptable by any standard.

Was the city officials more concerned about opening the Stock Exchange? as was rumored?

But then again, What was more important,? the publics health? Or making sure the economy didn't sink into a stock market crash? Hmmm. I wonder who tipped that scale.?

On Ground Zero there was a shortage of breathing respirators for the men and women that they had to use the cheap paper air mask filters and some didn't use them at all,

The better respirator mask were uncomfortable to use and hard to breath with because of the extreme heat on the surface but this was a situation that the respirator makers didn't expect when it was designed.

There was a shortage of them anyway so everyone reverted to paper filter mask which did not cover the smell of death and everything else that was burning.

Many workers decided to gamble and work without any mask so it wouldn't surprise me if a few years down the road in the not to distant future, these persons that didn't wear the proper face mask will probably begin to suffer serious respiratory problems.

The National Guard, manned all the boundaries, and it was at times kind of comical to see people turned away when they tried to talk these security personnel into letting them pass through. There were television crews from all over the world, China, Japan, France, England, Germany, Australia, Mexico, Canada, and several Central American countries, Peru, Argentina, Chile, and Columbia. and it seemed like everywhere I walked, I could here different languages being spoken behind me and in front. There were people from many different news crews with their giant white satellite dishes parked along the bay area, Transmitting news information all over the world.

The crowd, also consisted of Polish, Greek, Hungarian, Puerto Rican, and Cuban onlookers from the neighborhood.

But I was there to work and I had to find the recruiting station for volunteers, and in a place like New York City, it wasn't easy,

It seemed like every volunteer I met later ran into the same thing I did,

We were led to one place, then another, And some enforcement officers I'd ask just didn't know where the volunteer recruiting station was or if there was one in existence. Which made me wonder did they even want me to know?

All this walking and carrying my duffel bag with cloths and sleeping bag worked up a thirst so I stopped at a local Irish pub for a bite to eat and quench my thirst and if anyone stood out in the crowd, I did, With my bags, I sat down and waited for a waiter, and considering the situation in New York I suddenly realized that if I was a New Yorker, and I saw this stranger walk in and sit a couple bags down, with all these reports of terrorist going into restaurants and bars and blowing the place up,

I'd probably be looking at him, real suspiciously especially since I walked in carrying a couple bags.

Maybe that's why they were kind of looking at me the way they were.

But I relaxed and ordered dinner and a brew, and when I told them that I was there as a rescue volunteer from Indianapolis, Indiana, I could almost see them all breath a sigh of relief and their attitude seemed to turn to the friendly side.

They told me about the Jacob Javitz Center which was where all the recruitment for volunteers was, and they were more than glad to direct me there.

So I waved a cab down, and the cab dropped me off right in front of the place. When I arrived at the center I noticed a variety of different law enforcement agencies from several different states.

About three hundred officers mingled all over the place, from New Jersey, Massachusetts, Long Island, Queens, Bronx, Brooklyn, Newark, Staten Island, and even Ohio and that was just the beginning.

There were people walking in almost every direction from the center and it wasn't hard to find where the volunteer signup sheet was, as volunteers formed a line, and I wondered how many days they've had a line there.

My blood was pumping, and now I could feel the anxiety all the volunteers were feeling at that moment especially when we actually signed our name on the dotted line my hand was shaking,

It kind of reminded me of how the revolutionary civilians were feeling when they signed up as volunteers of the revolutionary army, after all, it was a war act that brought me here.

After we signed up everyone was ready to go, but all we had to do now, was wait until there was a background check made by the [FEMA] federal Emergency Management Agency, and possibly the FBI.

The Jacob Javitz Center was not only a recruiting signup station, But also the main location for all incoming donations of food, medical supplies, and various types of equipment that was needed for the workers of Ground Zero.

Every volunteer had to sign up the FEMA registration sheet with background information about yourself, and then, it was a waiting game, I couldn't believe the stack of applications on the table that were piling up so high, and the volunteers kept coming from all over the country.

But a large portion of these volunteers were going to be turned down, because anyone with a conviction in their past was not allowed to work as a volunteer and there were no exceptions.

America was responding to an emergency within our country and anyone with a criminal record, or conviction, wouldn't even be allowed to serve water, the only problem was that they didn't tell anyone that bit of information and I'm sure if they did, there wouldn't have been as many volunteers waiting around.

Security was tight, and in many ways it was very unfair not only to the person with a minor conviction in their past which was in some cases several years ago.

But I believe it was unfair to the victims that were buried because I'm sure they wouldn't have minded if these men had a minor conviction or not, They just wanted their bodies dug out of there and turned over to their families.

This was a national emergency and men were turned away who were equipped with the torch equipment and welding rigs that were badly needed to get the victims out.

The city needed and called out for torch tips and torch equipment which where badly needed and when men showed up with the equipment the city officials said we'll take your equipment but you were arrested several years ago for stealing a car so you can't come in to help. PS Tell me what was wrong with this picture.? The city still needed every able bodied man and woman that could stand the stress. People with the equipment were turned down including groups of Firefighters that had traveled from as far as Wichita Kansas. Others waited so long they felt like they were being turned away by being ignored.

Time was of an essence, and there were men there that no matter what they did in the past, They were now trying to do something sincere, and honorable, not just for themselves, and not for money, But for their country.

Some of these men worked as welders and had brought their own steel cutting equipment. Welders with steel cutting equipment were in big demand.

The main recruiting desk in front of the Javitz Center, was calling out for donated torch tips, and better quality respirators for the workers on the disaster site that needed them badly.

I personally couldn't understand why the City didn't furnish them, After all, this was a National Emergency.

Every man on Ground Zero was going to need one, I noticed later that there were men that refused to wear them because they were uncomfortable but it was not as uncomfortable as the respiratory problems they would likely have in the near future.

If there was contaminated air four blocks away, just how bad was it on the actual site? There were still fires raging underground so did toxic fumes surround that area?.

That first night I met some volunteers, Matt Linthieum from Cincinnati, Ohio, and Pops, and James, from Kentucky, There were people camping out on the side walk, and parking lot across the street from the Jacob Javitz Center, Matt invited me to join his group of friends, waiting it out., and we all got along great, we were all there for the same reason, Search and Rescue, or anything we could do to help this city.

Matt's pickup truck was parked across from the center, so we all stayed up late into the night since no one could sleep we all talked about where we were from and what made us decide to come here to New York,

There were volunteers from Alabama, Texas, Michigan, Florida, Georgia, Arizona, California, and Illinois, Everyone was so pumped up that, no one could sleep.

But soon I ended up on the back of the pickup bed in my sleeping bag, with the rest of the volunteers sleeping on the pavement all around the truck, and along the street.

That first night around 5;30 in the morning, I awoke from the sound of a man crying, and saying, [I can't believe this happened,] P.S. I didn't want to interrupt the conversation so I just tried to ignore it, and as the man continued crying he said, [I can't believe my people did this, Those were my people, that did this, I am ashamed of my people, and my religion.]

And that's when I sat up and realized I was almost face to face with a young Arab standing next to the truck bed and his eyes were filled with tears.

At first, when he turned and saw me, he started to walk away, But I called out to him and asked if he would like to talk as a friend.

He said his name was Ahmed, And he was so ashamed of what happened because the terrorist were Arab and he was ashamed of being an Arab because of what happened.

I don't really know why, but I stood up and climbed down to the pavement, and I walked up to him, and I put my hands on his shoulders, and I looked him in the eye and I said Ahmed, always be proud of your people, your customs and especially your religion, The people that did this were Not! of your religion.

They were only using your religion as an excuse for the brutality they inflicted on their own people, and on the people that stood up to them.

They have been hiding behind the name of your religion and they're not worthy of any paradise except Hell.

The men that did this were evil men, and there are evil men all over the world,

But evil can be fought with the good in our hearts and By believing in what is right and knowing when one is wrong.

So don't ever be ashamed of yourself, your nationality, or your religion because your religion has nothing to do with what happened, the people that did this do not deserve to be called Arab they are a satanic evil breed all by themselves and in America we call them demented scum of the earth Devils.

I even stuck my neck out and promised Ahmed that there would soon be peace in his country, Ahmed looked at me for the longest moment, And he said do you think it is possible? And I said, It's more than possible, It will happen.

Ahmed slowly took a deep breath and thanked me as he shook my hand gratefully, he thanked me over and over as he walked away, We never saw him again.

The next morning, everyone crossed the street to listen to the roster call, at 8;00 am, everyone was eager to do something to help.

One such guy walked up to me and handed me a large back-pack which contained a brand new torch outfit complete with gages, goggles, and all the proper accessories that was needed to cut steel and all I needed now were two tanks one with oxygen and one with Acetylene.

When I asked him why was he giving it to me, He said he knew my name would be called, he knew I was going in, and when I asked him for a return address so I could send it back to him when I finished, He said, don't worry about it,

Just use it and he walked away.

This guy was going home after waiting five days, he had a conviction in his past, and he realized he wouldn't pass the background check.

But what made it worse was the officials wouldn't tell us which of us didn't qualify, they wouldn't even bother to call your name and let you know that you didn't pass the back ground check so some guys waited days before finally giving up and going home.

This did build some resentment with some guys, simply because they waited so long for nothing.

This also built up the suspense, of waiting to be called on even more.

There was also another thing that was about to happen, that would soon effect all of us. The steel workers union was going to be granted the contract to remove the steel and rubble from ground zero, and soon the order was going to be given out to remove all non union volunteers from ground zero, when volunteers were called, there was first an interview, and then a pledged oath to the United States government, and each volunteer was issued a photo pass ID for the restricted areas, which all volunteers wore around our necks, Next volunteers were issued respirators and hard hats and given our schedule, either day or night shift, And upon reporting on schedule, volunteers then boarded the buses that transported all workers to Ground Zero,

The convoy of buses were escorted with police sirens wailing away and passing a parade of crowds that were cheering and waving flags, on the side of the streets and holding up signs that read THANK YOU, and GOD BLESS AMERICA, and WE LOVE YOU, and THANKS,

Soon the buses approached the Ground Zero area with armed National Guards at the check point., We could see the tremendous devastation that even at that time looked so unreal, Was this a dream? Were we all going to suddenly wake up from a nightmare, No one made a sound, Every worker could feel their stomach tighten up, not from fear, but from the combination of anguish, despair, helplessness, and a need for immediate revenge for what all workers were seeing at that moment, It was horrific, beyond description, but what struck fear in our hearts was the thought of what we were about to see up close.

As the buses pulled up, as near as they could go, Everyone was given final instructions and warnings then everyone calmly stepped off the bus and were stunned not only at the sight before us, But at the thought, that we had just stepped on to the disaster devastation of the century in America.

The smell of death, was in the air and everyone rubbed Vicks vapor-rub over their upper lip and inside of the respirators, to help withstand the smell of death.

Every worker hoped that we would find at least one survivor, We prayed in our hearts, for the sound of anyone's voice down below as we climbed up the concrete and steel pile of debris.

We just wanted to help, And it didn't matter what we had to do, Even if we had to get on the bucket brigade to help the firemen who had been working desperately to find their fellow Firefighter brothers that were still missing.

The Firefighters needed to rest, And we were ready for anything as we walked up closer to the ruins we were still a short distance from the actual area and even at this distance everything looked so, DESTROYED. Complete devastation and even with the respirators on you could still smell the massive pile of destruction.

It was horrific as the smoke rose from so many areas that it had an Erie effect on the scenery of the work area.

We could see the workers walking through the area with the bright giant Hollywood lights lighting up the place.

The workers were lifting, bending, pushing, and climbing and there were men giving orders and men giving signals for the cranes to lift sections of concrete which was when most of the time they would find the victims buried beneath.

We passed several Firefighters that looked like they could verily walk from their legs and feet being so sore, and many of the workers were covered with a chalky ash or powder one look into their eyes and faces told you the hell they had been through. It was almost a look of shock, disbelief, and trauma, all wrapped up in one package.

There were also triage tents with nurses administering first aid to the injured workers and a special triage tent specially set up for the injured Police search dogs who deserve credit for finding dozens of victims and body parts.

There were professional veterinarians to care for the Police dogs, with extra care.

There were still Firemen working the bucket brigade where they would ladder row chunks of concrete to the trucks that would haul them to the landfill.

The hours seemed to pass so fast and the weather seemed to be holding out for everyone. [Thank you Jesus] Sparks from the torches that were cutting steel and rod iron sections loose sparkled as the steel cutters worked non stop.

There was so much to cut that it seemed endless and we kept listening for anyone's voice down below the concrete sections.

Tears streamed from our eyes over our respirators from the anticipation and it was real sorrow at its worst, and many of us wanted to stop and dig with our hands, but everything had to be done orderly and by the numbers.

Everything had to be moved or cut away carefully to avoid cave-ins which is what happened to several Firefighters which were quickly dug out and lifted to safety.

There wasn't one volunteer that didn't shed a tear, not just for the victims, but for their fellow workers that expressed their feelings openly.

There was a look of complete exhaustion on everyone's face but the work kept going.

Our crew had only been on the site for eight hours when we were all called back to the bus we arrived in.

There was no explanation, just pack your gear and return to the bus quickly and immediately.

There was no explanation, Just orders to return to the bus immediately,. Everyone gathered their equipment, and boarded the bus, without saying a word, The heat was still unbearable and we just couldn't believe the destruction we saw in that short amount of time.

It seemed like the Federal people responsible with the actual recovery of the bodies were experiencing the toughest task of all, in identifying and processing each body, or body part that was found, tagged, and photographed. DNA tissue samples were taken if possible.

Each bit of information of every body was placed into a computer, including all description aspects of each victim, like what color of hair, cloths, jewelry, tattoos, the type of shoes, and scars or dental work.

This was then relayed to a central location where families would describe what their loved one was wearing that day, And if there was a hit on the computer, then it meant they had possibly found the body, which was tagged with a number and the location of the freezer truck that contained the body bag with that person, No information was given on the condition of the body, only that it was found, which in itself was a relief for most of the families.

The public soon even found out that the rescue workers had come across an infestation of rats, which became just one more problem in the search effort, The rats seemed to be coming from the main sewer and some workers reported thousands had been sighted within the ruins.

This seemed to be just one more problem to worry about for the workers.

We were told not to divulge this information but somehow the media got a hold of it and it was reported on the news in New York.

All ID tags that were issued to the workers were confiscated when everyone got off the bus.

Then we found out through the other volunteers that were listening to the radio, that the Steel Workers Union was now in charge, with a city contract to remove the steel and debris, and they wanted all volunteers removed from ground zero at once because now we were dipping into their piece of union pie.

So I salute all the volunteer workers that made it to New York City, to help, And it doesn't matter if you got to work or not, Its just the thought that you answered the call for your country that counts.

For the longest time, after volunteers were removed from ground zero, they felt this resentment towards the Steel Workers Union, for not allowing us to continue in the search.

Maybe it was an insurance liability reason, and maybe it was because the Union just wanted to employ their own union workers first, But there was nothing we could do, just follow orders, and pull out from the area it wasn't a humanitarian mission anymore, It was a multi-million dollar Union contract and they didn't want any volunteers in their work area.

After all, we were all there for humanitarian reasons and not for a paycheck.

This reminded me of the scale of justice, with, bureaucracy on one side, and humanitarians on the other.

At first they wouldn't let you work if you had a criminal conviction in your background but now if you had a Union steel workers membership card you were in.

You can bet your bottom dollar that the steelworkers were no virgins in the criminal department, And if they had turned down every steelworker that had a conviction in their past, I wonder how many steelworkers would have been left to work on Ground Zero.,

Did someone forget to mention, that this was a national emergency,? and the decision to allow someone to help dig out, and search for human lives, should not have been based on whether you had a union card?

My social security card identifies me as a tax paying American, and our presence there ready willing and able, should have been enough credentials to show that we deserved the chance to work with the city, for our country and for the victims that were buried in the rubble.

I remember walking to the steelworkers union hall # 40 in New York City, with fellow volunteers Matt, James, and others, to ask union leaders for special permission to work with their men,

And when we walked in the waiting room where some steel workers were waiting to be called, I took one look at them, and I could have sworn I had just walked into a prisoners probation office,

No, these were definitely not your everyday boy scouts., But then again boy scouts was not what you wanted at Ground Zero, they needed strong willed hardcore men that could finish the job at hand.

They may have been hard workers, But one thing they weren't, was sweet and innocent, With a spotless record,? The steel workers did an outstanding job and the work they were involved in was not for the meek, It took a strong heart and skilled person to do the things they had to do, and it couldn't have been done better by anyone else but the Steelworkers of America, They were the ones that built the World Trade Center so they deserve the honor to carry it out.

One of the first things I noticed as I approached closer the to ground zero area was a three block long row of emergency ambulances from several areas, QUEENS, BRONX, and MANHATTAN to name a few. their job was picking up body bags of the victims and delivering them to the temporary morgue.

When I arrived at the Jacob Javitz Center it seemed like chaos but FEMA organizers had it all well under control.

FBI Chopper pilots take a well deserved lunch break in front of the Javitz center.

Along the bay front television satellite dishes report and update news to the world.

A destroyed vehicle is towed to the barge that will take it to the **Fresh Kills Scrap yard on Staten Island.**

Brian McSherry though his appearance there was honorable and patriotic, he was an experienced steel worker with a complete welding rig was turned away because he did not hold a union card.

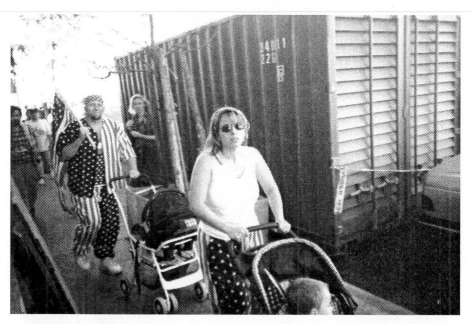

Patriotic couple and there baby gave the city fashionable moral support.

A Japanese reporter interviews me and asked me why I was there, And my answer was **BECAUSE I'M AN AMERICAN.**

One of five trucks donated by FED-EX with donated items that were needed by all the workers at Ground Zero Me and driver Vester Williams

As donated items were unloaded they had to be separated, sorted, and distributed.

Volunteers, John, [Jay, US Marine]   [Debbie, NURSE]. Rick. taking a break.

CHAPTER FOUR

NEW DAY, NEW JOB

While all the volunteers were still trying to figure out what they were going to do now, Matt and the guys had to go back to Ohio and the last thing I heard him yell out to me was I'll be back Rick in three or four days, and I said, Sure, We'll see, I never saw him there again, but James Tallant of Edgewood Kentucky did return and worked as a volunteer.

There were other sections of the rescue operation that needed volunteers,

The Jacob Javitz Center was being overwhelmed with thousands of tons of food, medical supplies, boots, socks, gloves, tee-shirts, sweat shirts and thousands of gallons of drinking water, respirators, blankets, fruit juices, sodas, fruits like apples, oranges, bananas and many more items that were desperately in need, including Teddy Bears and Beanie Baby's which we handed out to workers as a reminder to the workers that the country is thinking of them.

Many of the small beanie baby's were taped to the boots or carried in their pocket into Ground Zero.

A group of men from Fort Worth and Desoto Texas brought a huge smoking grill complete with a grinder to grind the meat and make sloppy Joe sandwiches, They brought six trucks and a flatbed

53

carrying mesquite logs, and 35,000 lbs. of 100 % pure Texas beef to grill on the steel grill,

But I was now stationed across the street, and our job was to unload all the supplies and then separate and organize items together, and distribute them to the various police, firefighters, and rescue personnel, and volunteers that needed them.

I ended up working twelve hour shifts with many other volunteers, and a couple times I ran into thieves, that had breached the area and were trying to steel articles that were meant for the Firemen, Police, Rescue and Volunteer workers only.

From there I was moved to the food area preparing snack bags, sorting bottled water, and filling cardboard boxes with Styrofoam covered food plates to send to the workers at ground zero,

One day I was handing out fruit juices and various types of drinks, when a lady passed by and I gave her a drink, And when she passed by I told a fellow worker, [That looked like Susan Sarandon] and she said, It is Susan Sarandon. Susan had taken the time out from her schedule to work in the food area, she was a very polite person, and everyone loved her.

Then on the 22nd and the 23rd of September, I had the honor of working with a group of people preparing food plates for the workers with MASH star, Loretta Swit.

Loretta Swit had taken some time out of her schedule to volunteer on the Texas grill.

Loretta Swit was not only looking great she was a very good worker and a very nice person to work with.

While she was grilling steaks, We were grinding it to make sloppy Joe sandwiches and sending out 350 to 450 plates at a time.

The Styrofoam covered plates had the American flag, with an eagle printed on top in red, white, and blue.

We needed more soft drinks and I was informed that there were cases in a semi-trailer across the street.

So I took some guys with me and on the way I asked a couple guys if they didn't mine helping unload some soda pop, since they were already in the restricted area, one of the guys said, [Certainly, we don't mind helping out] and then I realized one of the guys was Joshua Jackson, of the Dawsons Creek series.

He was with his step brother, and they both helped carry a few cases that were placed into 50 gallon drums with ice.

But just to see these celebrities stand by our side and helping in any other way they could, brought us all a little bit closer to reality, and down to earth, Because that is what they were, Down to earth, real people, And their presence there was like a shot of encouragement that we all needed.

Everyone knew that we were all there, because of a tremendous devastation, And that thought was always on the back of our mind.

The celebrities made us all feel like we were working together as family, and friends, Their presence there was greatly appreciated by everyone.

Then one day a group of guys were referred to a construction company that was hiring the laborers to work Ground Zero and they invited me to go with them.

We first called several times and I kept telling the guys there is something wrong because we kept getting the same recording [Sorry, we are temporally closed due to structural repairs] so I told the guys to call information and ask for the address and when they gave us the address everybody was surprised ONE LIBERTY PLAZA at World Trade Center,...We'll here we go again. Talk about structural repairs and temporally closed.

That location was permanently closed Heck the place don't exist anymore, at least not that main office.

Then I met a couple of guys that had dropped off donations from out of state and for some reason the driver [whose name I will not mention] was trying his darnest to acquire a security pass which most of us had to sign up and wait to be called, but for some reason he was as stubborn as a mule and more like a jackass.

He actually thought that FEMA officials were going to go through the complete process to grant him a security pass that he wasn't even going to use because he had to return to his home town to run a family owned business the next day. I've met some idiots in my life time but this guy deserves a crown for the king of idiots award. Yeah, you know who you are.

CHAPTER FIVE

HONESTY, IN NEW YORK

When I left Indianapolis to go to New York, I made the mistake of not writing down any one's addresses and not even my family knew I was going to New York.

So every one of the post cards and letters I sent home were addressed to my own residence, and my best friend Brenda Mazerolle would deliver them to my family and friends, She was also in charge of baby sitting my apartment while I was gone.

One morning I woke up and filled out four very large post cards I had purchased the night before, with the picture of the World Trade Center skyline, I filled them out which was like writing a long letter on the back of each one.

Then I placed them in my small notebook journal, and walked four blocks to the post office and every now and then I would glance down to make sure the cards were still there.

And when I stepped up to the counter, I reached for the four cards and only one was there, I looked all over for the other three cards, and I even walked back the four blocks to my hotel room, where I looked carefully and I still didn't find them, they were gone forever.

So I sadly walked back to the post office and mailed the postcard that was addressed to my son, Rico who works for UPS [United Partial Service] in Indianapolis.

I had excepted the fact that the other cards were lost forever. I went back to work that day and tried not to think about it.

Then about a week later, I went home, still wondering about them cards, and thinking who might have ended up with them then three days after I got home, the cards arrived in the mail, And on the back of one of the cards, someone had written in blue ink [I am a New Yorker, I found these cards and mailed them for Rick,] Then they drew a smiley face on it, And it wasn't until a day later that I noticed that someone else had written on that same card, this note, [I lost the guy I was seeing, and his brother, He was the captain of the FDNY, Painful for us all.] That card was addressed to my family, I couldn't believe that some one had taken the time to mail these cards for me, and now I have them. So to the people that found and sent the postcards home for me, Thank You, and God Bless. There is still honesty in New York.

Partial photo of postcard that was returned after it was lost with special sentiment notes added by two other people that were affected by the New York tragedy

Philip DeVan poses with fellow volunteers Susan Sarrandon and Mia Farrow

Another volunteer at the Javitz Center was Joshua Jackson, of Dawsons Creek along with his half brother helped unload soft drinks from a truck for the workers.

Reporting to work with fellow volunteer Marine, Jay DeFrank

Egyptian girls Oha and Galila with a television camera crew following them carry ice cold soft drinks for the workers.

Suspicious character is searched and found to have stolen items that were meant for the Firefighters and the other workers, He was not arrested.

Bar-be-que Grill was donated from Fort Worth Texas and drivers traveled from Desoto Texas with six trucks of equipment and a flatbed trailer with mesquite wood and 35,000 lbs, of 100% pure Texas beef, that was grilled for the workers of Ground Zero.

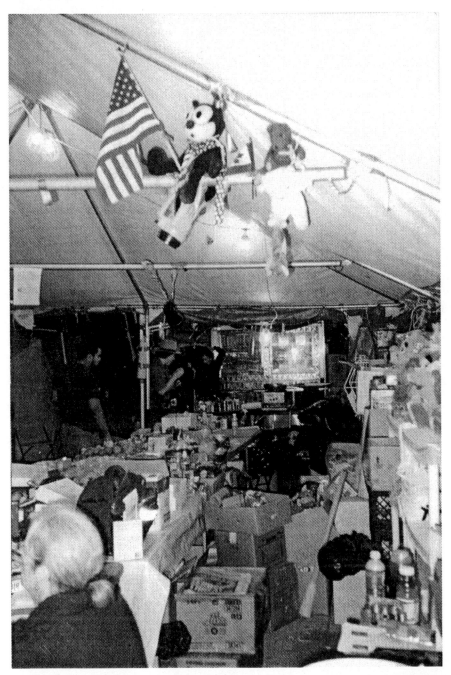

Inside tent loaded with supplies food snacks and every kind of drink you can think of.

Volunteers keep soft drinks on ice 24 hrs a day

Loretta Swit takes a break from the grill.

What was left of a Fire Chief's squad car

Chicago police officers assist Westhampton police officers pick up long sleeve T- shirts in Brooklyn ON October 2001.

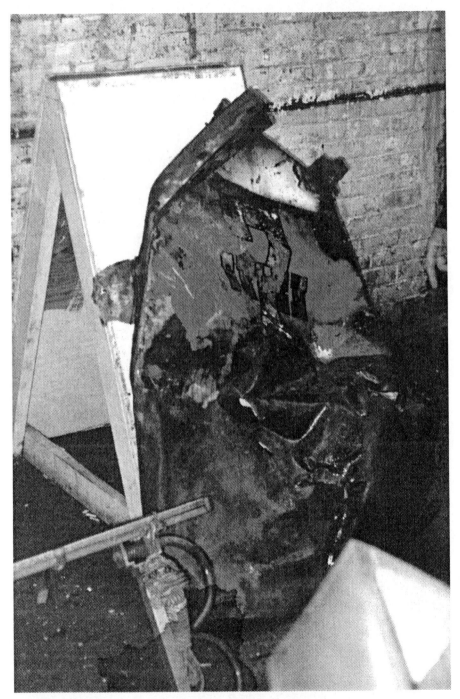

This is the door from # 7 Fire Truck dug out from the rubble.

Claw loaders load dump trucks at ground level and remains of victims are still being discovered December 2001.

Volunteers unload supplies

Thousands of people have passed by the signing wall to write their thoughts.

NYPD officers take a break after a long hard day.

What was left of a LEXES [left] and a MERCEDES [right] that was dug out from the rubble loaded on to a flat bed trailer.

Columed wall stands ready to be tore down.

Giant ramp workers walk down into Ground Zero. [cost three million dollars]

Four buildings stand damaged from towers falling down against them. Tallest building was ripped open when north tower crashed against it. [notice height of windows broken out in building in background.

Damaged vehicles wait to be removed

Elevator shaft is loaded on to barge near south street.

Author touches stone section broke off of South Tower.

Some of the hundreds of bags of dog food donated from across the country for the search dogs.

Trucks entering Manhattan are searched at check point.

Lower floor levels of fallen towers can be seen, Pathway subway tunnel at lowest level.—Also lookout platform for the public to look inside the work area is under construction

Lone steel beam with flag will be last piece of steel removed from Ground Zero area with a memorial parade procession

pictures say it all

At Saint Patrick's day parade Firefighter Cadets each carry 343 flags in honor of every Firefighter lost at the World Trade Center.

Firefighter statue will be mounted on to base with words to, America The Beautiful

A group from Kentucky donated this Fire truck to Ladder #10

Philip DeVan took part in inviting Olympian's to Fire station on Firefighters Day, and it made their day.

New world Trade Center design in the making at DDC Dept of Design and Construction.

Federal Building damaged from fallen North Tower across the street.

Philip devan poses with olympians Tom Samuel [Canadian Bobsled] Jim Shea USA Gold, Alison Stierle [Canadian Female Bobsled] and Todd Hayes silver medal

This one platform supported search lights, each with 1200 amps, and it took 82 lights to make one blue tower of light. [There were two towers of blue lights] From a Las Vegas light company

Firemen examine Todd Hayes silver medal at House 10

Steel beams imbedded into the building across the street from the World Trade Center still cling and hang from the building with the rubble still piled up below

Steel beams loaded on barge head for scrapyard—also destroyed vehicles from Ground Zero are piled up on Staten Island scrapyard

Philip and twin brother Dan DeVAN pose with [Boxer] Rinaldo Snipes

Emergency Rescue patches from Italy, and across the United States adorn the Recreation room of Engine #7 Ladder One, This is where CBS documentary was filmed.

Gold medallist Tristin Gale [left] Commander Pollareck and Silver medallist LeAnn Parsley

CHAPTER SIX

THE RESCUERS

There were people coming into New York from all over the country, to assist in the search and rescue efforts, And the public is not aware of the various ethnic nationalities that were involved and held in high esteem by the city and by the firemen in Ground Zero.

One such group was The Rescate Topos, [Rescue Moles] From Mexico City, these four men were led by Guillermo Suchil, who organized his search and rescue team in1985 after the earthquake that devastated Mexico City.

These men are trained professionals, that specialize in search and recovery. Each man paid their own way to New York, to help search for survivors, or items that would identify the bodies.

They have since traveled to 15 different disaster sites around the world, using their experience in search and rescue, in such places as Columbia South America, Hungary, Turkey, India, and Japan. They have been invaluable to rescue teams, and are highly respected around the world. At Ground Zero, They worked the twelve hour night shift co-ordinating their search efforts with authorities at the site.

Though their certification documents, luggage, and equipment were temporarily delayed, They were welcomed on board the USNS, Comfort.

This gigantic white ship with a giant red cross painted on it's sides, is a naval hospital ship, and was docked on the bay area just around the corner from the Javitz Center assisting with the first aid, temporary lodging, and preparing hot meals for the search team workers.

The Mexican rescue team was welcomed with open arms, The group of four men were given a place to rest, sleep, and enjoy warm meals.

Guillermo Suchil stated that his group would stay as long as they were needed, and then return home, to Mexico City.

THE OGLALA SIOUX TRIBE

Another rescue team that arrived at the Jacob Javitz Center was the Lakota Search and Rescue Team of the Oglala Sioux Tribe from the Pine Ridge, reservation in South Dakota.

Along the way one of the teams vehicles broke down in Belleforte, Pennsylvania, and at first the men didn't know what to do, They were in the middle of nowhere in an unfamiliar part of the country.

Then it happened, they were touched by the spirit of America.

Word got around about the Police Search and Rescue teams vehicle being broke down and the town helped them fix the vehicle at no charge, and sent them on there way to complete their mission. It was unbelievable, the people were so nice.

They were led by, Police Captain James Twiss of the Oglala Sioux Tribe, Department of Public Safety and upon arriving in New

York City they reported to the NYPD and were welcomed with open arms. Says Capt. Twiss, [We were treated great, by everyone and I would gladly go back if the opportunity came.

The people of New York were wonderful and treated the team with respect,].

Lt. Ortiz of the 18th District. Also helped and welcomed the Lakota Police Team and arranged quarters for them.

Captain Twiss and his men were assigned to special security responsibilities and other team members were assigned transporting and escorting food and supplies to Ground Zero.

These were true Indian Braves with their traditional long braided hair and black tee-shirt uniforms with white letters reading Lakota Police Search and Rescue, and EMS of Pine Ridge South Dakota...

They had volunteered to help their North American Brothers and Sisters in the search for survivors, and they had come a long way to help.

I felt proud to see them with their long braided hair and some wore what appeared to be ceremonial beads with claw.

This is what America is all about, they were the heart of America.

But the Lakota Police Team waited six days before deciding to return to Pine Ridge South Dakota, no one expected the background check to take as long as it did.

They had traveled over a thousand miles to assist in the search and rescue effort itself.

But one thing is for sure, They were a part of history just by being there and the special task which they were assigned to do was greatly appreciated by everyone.

The Oglala Sioux tribes of today and the future will now know that when this great country was in desperate need of volunteers in the most devastating destruction of property and human life in the history of America, The Lakota of the Oglala Sioux tribe of the Pine Ridge Reservation Search and Rescue Team was there ready, willing, and able.

It was the slow painstaking background check that was delaying many of the workers that were there to volunteer.

Though they may have returned to the reservation feeling a bit like they didn't do enough, they must remember that Hundreds of other volunteers that were pulled away felt the same way, but they did not waste precious time because time is endless, and has no value.

It was their presence there which was much more valuable because it is now recorded in history for their descendents in the future that will read this book and know there blood brothers and sisters were there.

The Oglala Sioux were a part of America United and the power of the people within America pulling together in the most historic time in history. We were one.

There is also one consolation,

The day the Lakota police left was the day the FEMA officers called out for the Lakota Police Team, So the Lakota Police and EMS were NOT rejected.

I myself was sorting donated materials when I heard the officials call out for the Lakota Police, and I spiritually called out to them [Where are you?]

The following are the names of Americas heros of the Pine Ridge Oglala Sioux Tribe Department of Public Safety of the Pine Ridge Reservation. Including their EMT's:

1. Captain James Twiss - Law Enforcement, EMT, Firefighter. S.A.R.
2. Dustin Baxter - Law Enforcement, EMT, Firefighter
3. Kieth Grube - Law Enforcement
4. Lance Fills Pipe - Law Enforcement
5. Bernardo Rodriguez - Law Enforcement
6. Dan Crazy Thunder - Law Enforcement
7. Robert Stover - Law Enforcement
8. Terry Demasters - Law Enforcement
9. Dennis Martinez - Law Enforcement S.A.R.
10. James Cottier - EMT., S.A.R.
11. Phillip Yellow Hawk - E.M.T., S.A.R.
12. Jay Youngman - E.M.T., S.A.R.
13. Davidica Youngman - S.A.R.
14. James Atchinson - E.M.T., S.A.R.
15. Phillip Clifford - Law Enforcement
16. Rob Menacher - E.M.T., S.A.R.
17. Jason Johnson - E.M.T., S.A.R.
18. Tom Janis - E.M.T., S.A.R.

19. Louise Pulliam - E.M.T., S.A.R.

20. Lexie Diaz - E.M.T., S.A.R.

21. Marquita Shields - E.M.T., S.A.R.

22. Angie Between Lodges - E.M.T., S.A.R.

And let's not forget the 300 search dogs from across the country that were used to search for victims, it was reported that at least two were killed in the line of duty at Ground Zero and they too will not be forgotten…

Capt. Robert Eads of TASK FORCE ONE Firefighters of Indianapolis signs one of two flags with the names of FDNY, PAPD, NYPD, FBI, and Search and Rescue personnel from across the country.

Donald Trump made an appearance at Robert DeNiro's restaurant TRIBECCA GRILL which was honoring five officers of NYPD precinct # 1, and five NY Firefighters of 10 House, Ivanna Trump hosted the event.

NYPD officer holds stuffed monkey sent from Eric of Kentucky to be given to a child.

CHAPTER SEVEN

THE TEDDY BEAR

As I walked through Times Square, during my time off with fellow Search and Rescue volunteer, Miguel A Gomez from Brooklyn, NY, He stated that even though there were not as many people on the street as there normally was, He said that the people were slowly coming back to the downtown area to, dine, and just hang out and walk the streets window shopping which was a New York past-time, for a lot of people.

Business was still only half as good as it was before, And life was slowly coming back to normal. We passed the Ed Sullivan Theater where David Letterman tapes his show and I told Miguel I just might write about being here in New York someday and one of these days I am going to go to the David Letterman Show because he is from my hometown.

I had heard that there were a lot of lights in New York, Times Square, But I never imagined what I would see, [Times Square New York, Your Incredible,]

One day after working a twelve hour shift, I happened to walk past a truck that was being unloaded with donations, and a young man was about to throw out a giant donated, Teddy Bear, that was wrapped in clear plastic, But the supervisor said get rid of it, It's to big,, and without a thought, He yelled [Catch!] And threw it at me, I caught it, just in time, and I said what am I going to do with it? I'm on my way back to the hotel and I'm walking, And he answered, [That's your problem now.] Now what am going to do,? The bear appeared new, or was well taken care of, and as I turned the bear around to see the front, I noticed that someone had written a message with a black marker, and it read,

[GOD BLESS AMERICA, WE LOVE YOU ALL,] and there was the name of the people who sent it Janet Jaggers and Thomas Vasko of Romulus Michigan with the address and the zip code And for the first time after seeing thousands of donated items come in, Here was a name and an address of the persons that sent it, And I suddenly felt personally blessed and related in friendship to these people for life, And they couldn't have found a better person to end up with the teddy bear.

But how was I going to carry it to the hotel, and back to Indianapolis, The bear was so big I was probably going to have to buy a bus ticket for it, Because it would have taken up a seat. And I sure wasn't going to ride the bus all the way home to Indianapolis with a giant teddy bear on my lap. So I took it back to the hotel room and kept it there, until I got ready to leave.

Hundreds of stuffed animals arrived as donations and many with personal notes of encouragement for the workers.

At Ladder Seven art work from Mrs. Pacheco's 2nd grade class at Taper Ave Elementary in San Pedro California hang on the wall with the following words [DON'T EVER GIVE UP HOPE JUST LOOK AT ALL THE BEAUTY IN LIFE.

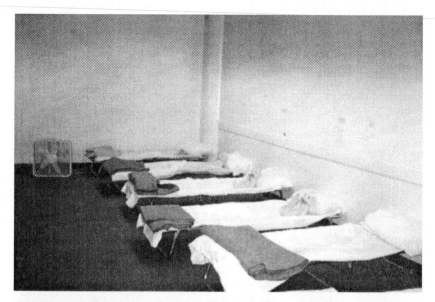

Teddy bears adorn all the cots at St Johns University where workers slept.

Group of River Rouge [DPW] worked on loading donations Rescue Bear can be seen on left back side.

Memorial park workers hold up new sign calling for donations

Rescue bear sits patiently waiting for his trip to New York

Janet Jaggers and Thomas Vasko and dog Tinker sent Rescue Bear.

Top - Truck loaded with donations from River Rouge and Romulus Michigan heads for New York City.

Bottom - Donations are unloaded in New York .

America and Religion United

Author stands with New Yorkers at Yankee Stadium Sept 23-01

CHAPTER EIGHT

AMERICA AND RELIGION UNITED

Then on September 23rd 2001, New York held a Sunday prayer service at Yankee Stadium, called, A PRAYER FOR AMERICA, to honor those who died in the World Trade Center disaster.

Oprah Winfrey was the master of ceremonies, and in attendance were former president Bill Clinton, Sen. Hillary Rodom Clinton, James Earl Jones, Archbishop of New York Cardinal Edward Egan, Boxing Promoter Don King, and the Boys And Girls Choir of Harlem sang, [We Shall Overcome],

Tenor singer Placido Domingo sang [Ave Maria,] And Beth Midler, sang the song that touched everyone's heart and brought tears to everyones eyes, [Wind Beneath My Wings,] touched everyone.

The crowd cheered when she sang the part, [You never knew, you were my hero] And unless you were there, You could never know just how emotional that part of the song was to everyone in attendance, Including Beth Midler herself, as she cried and hugged Mayor Giuliani, and Governor Pataki,

Beth hugged them both then walked back to the microphone and said, [Thank You New York, Thank You New York, Thank You]. Also Lee Greenwood was there to sing [God Bless The USA,] and it seemed like everyone in the stadium was singing parts of that inspirational song.

Thousands attended including church representatives from different faiths, Jewish, Catholic, Protestant, Muslims, Hindus, Sikhs, and Greek Orthodox, All united as one that day to not only pray for the dead, But to pray for America, it's allies, and the survivors.

Hundreds of police surrounded the area of the stadium inside and out, Every entrance and Exit was manned by two or more police officers, and every one that entered the stadium was searched.

There was a circular expensive floral arrangement made up of approx. three maybe even five hundred different floral arrangements bunched together in a circle around right field, After the service, ushers began to pick up each floral bouquet and carried them to the people in the stands. The YMCA ON 63rd and Broadway helped so many volunteers when we were basically street people until they came to our rescue, Miguel and I donated our flowers to the YMCA for their Lobby's.

We didn't expect this kind of shelter from Hotels and private residences that was offered free of charge to the volunteer workers.

This New York hospitality just blew us all away and it was nothing like we see in the movies, you don't get mugged on every street corner and you don't see police car street chases daily, not with this traffic, King Kong's fingerprints are not on the Empire State Building, and don't expect to see Spiderman swinging from building to building.

But New York is a spectacular city and so were the people, the skyscrapers, the ethnic choice of food, and the hospitality.

The volunteers appreciated the help from the people of the city more than you could imagine. Until that opportunity came to us, we were all feeling kind of helpless, because even though we didn't know where we were going to sleep or bath we were all going to help each other, any way we could, and we did, we were brothers and sisters till it was over, and friends for life.

The people in the stadium were all united in spirit. War veterans, some in wheel chairs handed out American flags. I attended the service with fellow volunteer Miguel A Gomez and we stopped just outside of the stadium before we entered to pray with a group of Hispanic missionaries, and that prayer was video recorded and televised on the religious program called The 700 Club, with Pat Robertson, I Just happened to be watching the program on the 24th or 25th of September when they were playing a song with a lady singing, and they were showing several scenes of New York, when suddenly, there I was, in red coveralls praying with a group of people on the street.

Later once inside we were met in the stadium by Marc J Ameruso of MJA Productions, which is a television film documentary company.

Marc and Miguel both met just hours after the Towers came down and they started pulling victims out of the rubble, risking life, and injury to themselves.

Miguel, Marc, and I, were directed to seats right in the front roll of the stadium along the right field line. Right in front of dozens of cameramen, from news media all over the world.

There were dozens of news paper, magazine, and television cameras and reporters recording the event, and it was televised on National television, Possibly world wide.

Every representative of each religion in attendance got about five minutes to say something about the disaster, followed by a prayer.

It was an emotional event for everyone, But the one prayer that moved me the most was when Iman Izak-El M Pasha, a police chaplain and spiritual leader of Harlem's Massaged Malcolm Sahibs Mosque, read from the Koran.

Even though I didn't understand a word he said, I felt, every sad emotion as he chanted the verses of the Koran, You could actually feel the sorrow in his voice just by listening, and watching him on the big screen within the stadium.

I guess it wasn't the words, It was the emotion, of the prayer. That touched me, The service ended with Billy Joel singing [I'm Proud To Be An American]

Crowds gather at Yankee Stadium for the Prayer for America memorial which was televised nationwide.

Mayor Rudy Guiliani blows a kiss to the crowd before leaving.

Reunion at Times Square with fellow Volunteer Miguel Gomez who is also a dedicated volunteer Firefighter.

Ground Zero sleeping quarters for workers near shipyard.

Emotional cartoon by Gary Varvel of Indianapolis Star and News depicts the agony, sadness, and political emotion felt across the country.

[By permission of Gary Varvel and Creators Syndicate Inc, copyright 2001]

Members of task force One pose with flag signed by New York Rescue workers, Left- Mario Garza public information officer, 2nd Terry Toffolo[Engineer] Author Rick Espinoza and Capt. Robert Eads.

CHAPTER NINE

HOME BOUND

The day that I was heading home, I called a taxi, and the driver, Luis Medrano was shocked when he saw the giant teddy bear, and all the other things I was carrying, My sleeping bag, which was rolled up, with a donated comforter blanket that was also a large bundle.

Then I had the back pack with the torch equipment, and my blue duffel bag with my cloths, Luis drove me first to the Fed-X, who referred me to Mail-Boxes ETC, And when the cashier at Mail - Boxes Etc realized I was a volunteer heading back home, the attendant Jim Duggan informed me that they were going to ship the teddy bear and the large bundle of blankets Free of charge, and he stated that they were very grateful to the volunteers that had come to New York from so far away and for everything we've done for their city, Mail Boxes ETC, Shipped my belongings free of charge through UPS and I will forever be grateful, Mail Boxes ETC, I love you. Thanks.

The Taxi driver Luis Medrano didn't charge me for the ride, not even to the bus station, But I have his address and he'll be hearing from me again soon.

The whole city of New York was very appreciative of all the volunteers from out of town.

Everyone was very courteous to us, especially when they realized we were volunteers. My bus pulled out of the station that night at 6;30 p.m., September 2001, and as we pulled away from the Terminal, I thought about all the wonderful New Yorkers that welcomed all the volunteers with open arms.

I thought of all the brave and gallant men from the FDNY, NYPD, PAPD, The EMS medical teams, that signed my American flag, The FEMA Dog Search Teams, like Janet Linker and her Terrier, RICKY, and Fred Golba and his eight year old German Shepherd, AMO, Who found at least 44 bodies, or remains during the search, NYPD officer Veronica Hammer and her dog Smitty, and NYPD officer Paul Geltin and his Police dog Bandit, And Brittany another golden retriever that did her share in the search effort and the French Rescue team, Also the FBI who signed my helmet, the Sheriffs, Marshals, and the Red Cross Volunteers like Mary Richardson of Amarillo Texas, who also signed my American flag And the Steelworkers working 24 hours a day with the firemen, The Steel Workers deserve a lot of credit for the work they did, The men were just caught up in the political decisions that were made, They still had a job to do, and they did it well. And lets not forget all the out of state Firemen, like Captain Robert Eads, Terry Toffolo, Mario Garza, Mike Reeves, who were just a few of the members of Task Force One Firefighters, from Indianapolis, Indiana, who reported within 48 hours after the Towers came down, Several of these firefighters also signed my flag.

And all the other various police dog search teams form all over the country,

There were at least 300 search dogs on Ground Zero, and some carried special cameras as they climbed underground, and gave everyone above, a view of what was below the area they couldn't get to. The search dogs deserve a lot of credit for finding a lot of victims bodies in the ruins.

And I thought of all the priest of different faiths that gave the last right to the dead, And I, along with all the other volunteers were ever so grateful to Governor George Pataki and Mayor Rudy Giuliani, and everyone that was responsible for welcoming all volunteers to their Hotels and private residences, to rest, sleep, and bath.

There are no trophies, awards, certificates, or medals, that can equal the prestige of honor that these people and the search dogs deserve.

I will never forget New York City and all my new friends from all over the country.

And just as my bus drove into the Lincoln Tunnel, I looked back at the magnificent skyline of Manhattan, New York City, and I noticed all the skyscrapers standing straight, tall, and powerful together, with a full sky of gray clouds hovering just over the structures.

But what stood out most of all, was the Empire State Building towering far above all the other sky scrapers, and disappearing far into the clouds. Once again the Empire State Building is the tallest building in New York City, Once again New York City will rebuild like a giant picking himself up, and brushing himself off, Standing stronger and more powerful than ever. I love New York and my

Country, I was proud to represent the Hispanic community, and the people of my home state, and my home town of Indianapolis, And all the people that wanted to help but couldn't go.

CHAPTER TEN

REMEMBER TEDDY?

PS, Remember the teddy bear, that was thrown at me from the truck? well, It finally arrived a few days after I arrived home, His new name is RESCUE BEAR.

Several days later, after I had a chance to settle down, I tracked the phone number of the people that had sent the teddy bear, through information.

Janet Jaggars, and Thomas Vasko, but they weren't home, so I left them the following message, [Hello, my name is Ricky Lee; calling from Indianapolis Indiana, and I just got home from New York, from working as a volunteer, and on behalf of all the volunteers and Firefighters and rescue personnel, I'd like to thank you and everyone that was responsible for sending the truck with donated items, Everything you sent was used and appreciated, and Oh, by the way, I'm the one that ended up with your teddy bear.] I left my phone number, and soon after, I received their call, and we are planning a teddy bear reunion in the spring, GOD BLESS AMERICA.

CHAPTER ELEVEN

HOMECOMMING

When I returned home to Indianapolis, I was amazed at the way people within the city greeted me, and approached me to thank me for going to New York to help, Even strangers that had recognized me from the TV interview with our local news station that was in New York reporting the story.

It seemed everywhere I went in Indianapolis, I felt a sense of pride every time I saw an American flag waving on a car antenna, flag pole, window, home, or office building.

I also realized that this was just a fragment of American pride that still exist in America and it's always been there like a sleeping Giant its just a shame that the sleeping giant must be awakened with a tragedy to become aware that American pride, unity, and solidarity is alive and well. We should work together on building a bond of strength that no enemy can destroy or break down.

Together we are one, AMERICA UNITED.

Even in my fathers voice, I could tell how proud he was of me, when he would tell his friends that I had taken part of the volunteer operation in New York.

Like countless other volunteers that were there, I only wish I could have done more, But there was only so much we could do,

If not for the volunteers, that left there loved ones at home, to assist the City when they were down, New York City would have been in serious trouble with the thousands of tons of donated items that were transported there, When I got home I lit a candle in memory of all the victims of the world Trade Center disaster, And I guess Dorothy said it best, when she said [There's no place like home,] But she forgot, there's no place like America.

THE END

Back home with donated Rescue Bear

ABOUT THE AUTHOR

Born and raised in Indianapolis, Indiana October 17, 1952 to Feliciano and Maria Balli Espinoza with six sisters and one brother.

Never married, Rick is also a song writer and creative musician, commercial artist, loves horses, dogs, cats, aquariums, exotic foods, traveling, singing, fishing, riding his motorcycle, relaxing by the fireplace and living in the country.

I've always tried to follow in my fathers foot steps by being involved with social issues within our community that needed to be addressed and by helping others less fortunate whenever possible.

Americans in New York were buried alive and slowly dying and I knew that with that magnitude of destruction, even the NY

Firefighters, and rescue personnel were going to need every able-bodied man and woman that could help.

When interviewed in New York City by a TV news channel from Indianapolis and asked why I was there?

I responded "I have family in Ground Zero, The people buried and the people digging them out, their Americans, and so am I, that's why we're all here to get our family out."

Author can be reached at: ricardoyapa@yahoo.com

To Richard Reeve

Just thought I'd
let you know. the
guy you interviewed
in NY during Sept 2001
ended up writing a book
about the volunteers.

God bless
Never Forget
9-11-01

Printed in the United States
1046900005B/184-393